WOODS

WOODS

A CELEBRATION

ROBERT PENN

National Trust

Published in 2017 by
National Trust Books
43 Great Ormond Street
London WC1N 3HZ
An imprint of Pavilion Books Company Ltd

ISBN: 9781911358114

A CIP catalogue record for this book is available
from the British Library.

25 24 23 22 21 20 19 18 17
10 9 8 7 6 5 4 3 2 1

Reproduction by Rival Colour UK
Printed by Toppan Leefung Printing Ltd, China

This book can be ordered direct from the publisher
at the website: www.pavilionbooks.com, or try your
local bookshop.

INTRODUCTION

There is something precious about a collection of trees gathered together in a wood. There is a closeness, a wildness, an antique allure and a sudden intense spirit of place, which in concert can have a profound effect on us.

Walk a little way into a wood and there is a sense of things being different: you are cut adrift, in a realm of make-believe. The best woods are a mix of the solid and the evanescent, a compound of growth and decay, a blend of the timeless and the momentary, and a marriage of the very ordinary and the heart-stoppingly exquisite.

Broad-leaved woodlands resonate most strongly with us: among aspen and birch – the first species to colonise the land after the last Ice Age, some 10,000 years ago – amid cathedral-tall beech and ruler-straight ash, in the company of hazel, holly, hornbeam, alder, lime, wild cherry, horse chestnut and our beloved oaks, we feel a peace that is increasingly illusory in the modern world. In broad-leaved woodlands, nature is also at its richest: wild flowers, butterflies, lichens, mosses, moths and a plenteous mix of birds and mammals all thrive in well-managed woodlands.

Left: Dawn breaks on Hindhead Common in the Surrey Hills. This landscape, a rich mosaic of heathland and ancient woodland, was saved from further road development in 2011, when the A3 was diverted through a tunnel beneath the hills. From the natural amphitheatre of the Devil's Punch Bowl, there are extravagant views over the heavily wooded Weald.

By 'wood' or woodland', I mean a plot of land on which trees have grown in the natural course of things. In modern usage, it is a loosely defined term and might include spinneys, stands, copses, combes and thickets. On the other hand, orchards, avenues and parkland all have trees, yet nothing of the quality of woodland and are outside the definition, as are 'forests'. In the past, the term 'forest' did not necessarily imply an area of land covered in trees, while today it tends to be applied to an area of trees larger than a woodland, often primarily managed for the production of timber.

Though they sometimes look untouched and feel wild, it is important to remember that woodlands are the result of the interaction between our activities and natural processes over millennia. The successive crops of trees that resulted from these activities have provided wood and timber to meet a huge variety of fundamental human needs. From Mesolithic times until the end of the nineteenth century, we depended on wood – for fuel, building materials, furniture, domestic utensils, tool handles, transport and the manufacture of military equipment, to list just a few of the thousands of uses. Over that period, woodlands figured significantly in the lives of the vast majority of British people, culturally, symbolically and economically. In the last 100 years, imported timber, cheap coal and man-made materials like plastic have steadily reduced demand for domestic woodland products. Meanwhile, we have drifted *en masse* to cities. The role of woodlands in our daily lives has declined dramatically. Yet, in Britain's conception of itself, the myth of the heavily wooded island still looms as large as ever.

Left: Sessile oak trees in Gentles Copse on Ludshott Common, east Hampshire: woodlands like this are the result of the interaction between human activities and natural processes over millennia. Above: Fencing posts from a coppice woodland in the Surrey Hills. From Mesolithic times until almost the present, we depended on wood to meet a variety of fundamental human needs.

The National Trust is the second largest woodland owner in the UK. The organisation is custodian of some 420 individual woods, from Cumbria to Cornwall and Snowdonia to Suffolk, amounting to roughly 64,250 acres (26,000ha). This portfolio includes a great variety of woodlands, from the exotic, planted conifer woods at Cragside in Northumberland to the commercial beech stands at Ebworth in Gloucestershire, and from the prehistoric western sessile oak woods at St Mary's Vale in Monmouthshire to the newly planted woodlands on the Slindon Estate in West Sussex.

At the heart of the portfolio is a wealth of what is known, in silvicultural argot, as 'ancient woodland' – places in England and Wales that have had continuous tree cover since at least 1600. In terms of biodiversity, ancient woodland is extremely important. In fact, no other component of the British landscape is quite so valuable ecologically, both above and below the ground. Over the course of the last century, for a variety of social and economic reasons, including the effects of war, we felled and grubbed up vast swaths of ancient woodland, rendering what is left even more precious. Fortunately, the National Trust is engaged in both the sensitive management and, in certain locations like Fingle Woods in Devon, the restoration of ancient woodland.

Above: A carpet of ramsons (wild garlic) growing in Ebworth Woods, part of the Ebworth Estate in the Sheepscombe Valley near Stroud in Gloucestershire. The National Trust is custodian of these, and of some 420 individual woodlands across the UK.

The publication of this book coincides with the thirtieth anniversary of the Great Storm of 15 and 16 October 1987 – the most dramatic, single event in recent meteorological history, and a night that did untold damage to National Trust properties across south-east England. The hurricane-force winds reached 110mph (177km/h) and caused eighteen deaths, while the transport network collapsed and some three million houses were hit. The total insurance bill came to over £1 billion. The greatest cost, however, was to trees and woodlands.

The ferocious gale arrived with disastrous timing: after several days of rain, the ground was soft, while the mild autumn temperatures meant the trees were still heavily laden with leaves. In just a few hours, fifteen million trees were thrown down. Sevenoaks in Kent became 'Threeoaks'; historic woodlands and arboretums in Suffolk, Sussex and Kent were destroyed.

On National Trust properties alone, some 360,000 trees were blown over. The epicentre of the storm was around Greensand Ridge, a heavily wooded sandstone escarpment bordering the

Weald in Kent. At Emmetts Gardens, the National Trust garden and arboretum, almost all of the mature trees were either blown down or had to be felled except one notable survivor – the giant redwood, still standing proud. At Toys Hill, a National Trust woodland on the escarpment, some 95 per cent of the trees were razed.

In the immediate aftermath of the storm, many woodlands were machine-cleared and then replanted, at great expense. As the years passed, however, foresters, woodland managers and alone often fared better than those where there was intervention. Allowed to replenish itself, nature does a good job. It seems remarkable, but after thousands of years, our understanding of woodlands is still evolving.

This page: An aerial view of fallen trees in woodland on the Bradenham Estate in the Chilterns, Buckinghamshire following the Great Storm of 15 and 16 October 1987. In just a few hours, fifteen million trees were thrown down in south-east England: on National Trust properties alone, some 360,000

'A wealth of things indicate how the wheel of the year gently turns ... Trees mark the passing of time in their seasonal change'

This book is divided into four seasonal essays, of photographs and prose. We are not unique in having four seasons in Britain, but it is something to be celebrated. Most of the world's population live in the tropics and subtropics where there are only two seasons – wet and dry.

The best place to observe the changing seasons in Britain is, of course, in our woodlands. A wealth of things indicate how the wheel of the year gently turns – from ground flora and butterflies to beetles and fungi. Most obviously, the trees guide us through the seasons: by budding and leafing in spring; weaving the woodland canopy in the soundless days of high summer; putting on a sumptuous show of colour in autumn; and then standing bare and fragile through winter. Trees mark the passing of time in their seasonal change, reminding us that life passes and encouraging us to live well now.

Right: A red deer hind (our largest species), silhouetted at dawn. In autumn, if you are up early and lucky, there is a chance of witnessing the deer rut in woodland.

People are often surprised to learn that the UK is one of the least wooded countries in Europe, and it has been for a millennium. Of the 27 million acres (almost 11 million hectares) surveyed for the Domesday Book, only 15 per cent was wooded. Today, we have around 12 per cent woodland cover – well below the European average. Add climate change and the globalisation of tree pests and diseases to this state of affairs, and the future for our woodlands looks desperately uncertain. In this over-populated, over-ordered and over-civilised country, we need, as a society, to rediscover the importance of woodlands – as functioning components of the rural economy, as hubs for nature and perhaps most significantly, as places for us to feel less orphaned from the earth. Above all, we need to rediscover our reverence for the wonder of trees. To the woods!

Above: Beech trees draped in snow on Crickley Hill, a spur of the Cotswold Escarpment in Gloucestershire overlooking the Severn Vale. On a good day, there are grand views west towards May Hill and the mountains of Wales. The beech trees here were planted in the eighteenth century, but archaeological evidence shows human activity on the site goes back to 4,000 BC.

SPRING

'... with gentle hand

Touch – for there is a spirit in the woods'

—————

Nutting, William Wordsworth

'its arrival
is a joy common both
to us and to our forebears,
who walked through
the same woods hundreds,
perhaps thousands,
of years ago'

Observing the coming of spring is a fascination as old as the seasons themselves, and part of the British condition. There is a primitive satisfaction in knowing that its arrival is a joy common both to us and to our forebears, who walked through the same woods hundreds, perhaps thousands, of years ago. For meteorologists, who like to organise the year into four neat sections, spring begins smartly on 1 March. For astronomers, the vernal equinox – around 20 March – marks the true turning of the seasons. For some, it's the moment the clocks go forward. For trout fishermen, it's the first hatch of March browns. For my wife, it's when it's warm enough to hang the washing outside. For others, the herald of spring is equally personal: a pied wagtail over ploughed land; the first cut of grass; a dashing, yellow daffodil; the sound of a song thrush; creamy white flowers lighting up a blackthorn thicket; the earliest appearance of frogspawn in ponds; a brimstone butterfly on the edge of a woodland clearing; each of these events signals the arrival of spring for someone.

Signs of spring (clockwise from top left): The bright yellow trumpets of wild daffodils; frogspawn; a brimstone butterfly with its distinctive leaf-shaped wings; the creamy-white blackthorn flowers, which appear in March before the leaves.

For me, to feel that spring has truly sprung, to experience the deep surge of energy that the season so often releases, I need to see a pristine, unfurled, lime-green tree leaf. One of the earliest trees to leaf is the horse chestnut. It is not a common woodland tree, but the buds – large, reddish-brown and coated in a sticky gum that protects them from insects and frost damage – are easy to identify. When they burst, the succession of overlapping scales fold outwards into a rosette and the new shoot, covered in a fleece of white hair, emerges. Further shoots grow out of the main spike and the leaves – limp and greenish-white at first – unfurl from there, gradually strengthening and changing colour in the spring sunshine.

Large, extravagant and dandyish, horse-chestnut leaves are something to behold when they have reached their full potential. There are usually five or seven unstalked, elliptical, saw-toothed leaflets radiating out from a central point. The horse chestnut tree also grows flamboyant, bell-shaped flowers in spring. More famously, in autumn, the tree produces conkers, much loved by leagues of schoolchildren with grubby knees in a bygone era.

Sadly, today the horse chestnut is widely affected by a tiny moth – the horse chestnut leaf miner, which causes brown blotches to appear on the leaves in summer – and also a fungal rust, which results in discoloration on the tips and margins of the leaves in early autumn.

Left: Horse chestnuts are one of the first common native trees to leaf, usually in early spring.
Above: Though not a common woodland tree, horse chestnuts are easily identified by their large, extravagant leaves comprising five or seven saw-toothed leaflets.

It is difficult to be exact about the order in which our different, common woodland tree species burst into leaf every year. There are many determining factors – the age of the trees, the geographical location and orientation of the woodland, where a particular tree is within that woodland and even the origin of the tree seed. Generalising hugely, elder and horse chestnut are among the earliest to leaf, often in March. Sycamore, hawthorn, rowan, silver birch and field maple tend to come next, in a batch.

Perhaps a week after that, pedunculate oak trees leaf, then beech, followed by sessile oak towards the end of April. Ash is commonly the last of our native trees to leaf. The old English weather adage – 'oak before ash, we're in for a splash; ash before oak, we're in for a soak' – is, by the way, nonsense.

This page: Fresh, lime green foliage on an old oak tree on the Ashridge Estate in the Chiltern Hills, Hertfordshire. English or common oak is the most common tree species in the UK and one of the last to leaf in spring.

Robert Marsham, a Norfolk squire, first began recording the dates on which different trees come into leaf in 1736. He also noted down 26 other seasonal occurrences – tree flowering and blossoming dates, the first appearance of butterflies, the earliest singing cuckoo and so on – and compiled the data in what he called his 'Indications of Spring'. Marsham kept these records for 62 years. Successive generations of his family then continued to keep the records until 1958. This field of research, called 'phenology' – the study of the times of recurring natural phenomena – is arguably more important today than when Marsham lived, because of the insight it provides into the effects of climate change.

It seems that our changing climate is incrementally altering the occurrence of the signs of spring in our woodlands. Not everything is leafing and flowering earlier though, as you might expect with rising temperatures. Research appears to show that warmer autumns are having the opposite effect on some tree species. Using the record that was started by Robert Marsham in conjunction with more recent data, phenologists are now predicting a reshuffle of the order that trees in our temperate forests will leaf. This will inevitably have implications for the biodiversity in woodlands, and in particular, wild flowers.

Above: Apple blossom at Cotehele, Cornwall: spring sunshine encourages the flower buds of apple trees to swell and flush with pink, before the pure white flowers burst open.
Next page: Among the myriad changes happening to trees as the weather warms, blossom emerging is one of the most obvious and beautiful indications that spring has arrived.

Something that resembled a blue arrow had disappeared round a bend in the River Teign before I realised it was a kingfisher. This was my reward for rising early. I walked on, over the granite packhorse bridge, through the stone remains of a nineteenth-century corn mill, up the side of the gorge and into a pleat of the hill, as ribs of sunlight began to reach down through the trees.

The Teign Gorge is a staggeringly lovely part of Devon. The two arms of the river rise on Dartmoor and join forces before crashing through the steep-sided, tree-mantled gully beneath the National Trust property, Castle Drogo. I had come in early spring to visit Fingle Woods, 825 acres (334 hectares) of woodland acquired jointly by the National Trust and the Woodland Trust in 2013. In an unprecedented initiative, the two organisations are trying to repair the site – by removing the conifers that were planted during the twentieth century, and returning it to deciduous woodland. No one has ever attempted a woodland restoration project on this scale before.

Left: The steep-sided, tree-mantled Teign Gorge beneath Castle Drogo, with panoramic views south-west to the barren, windswept heights of northern Dartmoor.
Above: Fingle Bridge over the dashing River Teign, where the National Trust and the Woodland Trust have embarked on an ambitious, long-term ancient woodland restoration project.

The gorge first became a popular beauty spot in Edwardian times – the construction of Castle Drogo began in 1911 – but human occupation of this heavily wooded area goes back much further than this. There are three Iron Age hill forts on eyries high above the river. For some 500 years, up to the end of the nineteenth century, the area was intensively managed as a working woodland providing oak and other species for a variety of rural industries, particularly charcoal making.

During the second half of the twentieth century, though, great tracts of what now comprises Fingle Woods were clear-felled of broad-leaved trees and replanted with imported conifers. Sadly, the same thing happened all over Britain, on hundreds of other sites previously covered in what is known as 'ancient woodland' – places in England and Wales that have had continuous tree cover since at least 1600. Government policy during this era, especially between 1945 and the mid-1970s, was to grow timber fast, to make money and provide a strategic reserve for the nation in times of critical need. The policy was driven by economics and national security, not by conservation.

This page: A conifer plantation on the Castle Drogo Estate, Devon. In the second half of the twentieth-century, great tracts of ancient woodland across Britain were clear-felled of broad-leaved trees and replanted with conifers, destroying a variety of invaluable habitats. We now understand the error of this policy, but restoring these ancient woodlands will take decades.

In areas where the conifers have already been cleared, there were brambles and birch saplings as well as the first signs of several species of woodland flora – wood rush, violets and St John's wort among them – that will have lain dormant as seeds in the soil for decades, only springing to life again recently when the Douglas firs above them were felled.

Further down the river, I came to Cod Wood, a large stand of beech planted for timber in the 1930s, and now part of the Fingle Woods project. In the meek sunlight at the bottom of the gorge, the storm-grey branches and twigs contrasted dramatically with the first fresh, lime-green leaves.

Pleated, covered in silky hair and soft to touch like tissue paper, young beech leaves are a minor marvel of natural engineering. From a distance, they looked like random paint splashes. Beneath the beech, the woodland floor was illuminated by hundreds of wild daffodils – native, rare, more delicate and prettier than their planted cousins, wild daffodils are one of my favourite flowers.

Left: Wild daffodils, here surrounding the trunk of an aspen, are native, rare and prettier than their planted cousins.
Above: Wild daffodils are easily identified by their pale yellow petals and darker yellow trumpets; they are also shorter than planted daffodils and form in clumps.

'The spectacular British woodland wild flower show starts at the beginning of March, rising like a clarion call from the soil, summoning us to the woods'

The spectacular British woodland wild flower show starts at the beginning of March, rising like a clarion call from the soil, summoning us to the woods. Many of these flowers have to appear in early spring, to beat the heavy shade the canopies of the broad-leaved trees will soon cast. Fortunately, wild flowers grow abundantly in our old woodland, so you don't have to go far to witness the extravaganza. The list of National Trust woodlands worth visiting at this time of year is as long and varied as the inventory of wild-flower species they are home to. At Leigh Woods, above the Avon Gorge on the outskirts of Bristol, a host of rare flora appears on the limestone rocks and under the stag-headed oaks, the yew and the wild service trees. At Hardcastle Crags, near Hebden Bridge in the Pennines, West Yorkshire, greater stitchwort and bluebells show under the ash and the beech. In the extensive woodlands surrounding the famous, formal gardens at Nymans on the High Weald in West Sussex, you will find primroses, yellow archangel and dog violets.

Four of our woodland flowers (clockwise from top left): Greater stitchwort, with its distinctive deeply notched petals; the primrose, one of the first flowers of spring; yellow archangel, which looks like a nettle but doesn't sting; and the common dog-violet.

Timing, however, is everything. As with the unfurling of tree leaves, different species of wild flowers emerge from the earth at different times, in successive waves that are repeated across the country, year after year. Precisely when you go to the woods in spring determines what you will see. Lesser celandines usually provide the curtain-raiser on the show. Because they are common and grow almost anywhere, celandines have never scooped the acclaim they deserve – for breaking out early and doing so with conviction. If the winter lingers on, their butter-yellow petals provide a brilliant dash of colour when the rest of the landscape remains drab and grey.

Primroses, which flower in a variety of yellow shades on a bed of crinkled leaves, come early in March too, providing one of the first sources of food for bees, along with lesser celandines and ground-ivy. Next up are the wood anemones: white and pure, they sometimes occur in great, uniform carpets in ancient woodlands. In fact, because they spread so slowly, wood anemones are considered by historians to be a reliable indicator of ancient woodland. With white petals set around

egg-yolk yellow anthers, wood anemones are also easy to recognise.

By the middle of March, many woods are swamped by a sea of green as dog's mercury, green and stinking hellebore and, in particular, the leaves of bluebells emerge. Other types of woodland with different dominant tree species might have spreads of wild daffodils, woodland violets and oxlips around the same time. In the next act of the show, there could be swaths of ramsons, which form dense, garlic-scented colonies in the damp corners of ancient woodlands, or daubs of yellow

archangel and pools of greater stitchwort. At this stage, though, by the beginning of April, the wild flower that has the power of Prozac on the British collective consciousness is ready to make its grand entrance.

Above: Ramsons in woodland at Newark Park, Gloucestershire. When ramsons grow as extensively as this, your nose will identify the plants even before you see them, especially in April and May when they flower.
Next page: A lagoon of bluebells on the Ashridge Estate, Hertfordshire. As bluebells reproduce very slowly, by multiplying their bulbs, they are a valuable indicator of ancient woodland.

The bluebell is native and common throughout much of Britain. It does grow in hedgerows and meadows, but you scarcely notice it there. In deciduous woodlands, however, bluebells are a natural wonder, and a gift that is almost unique to the Atlantic realms of Western Europe.

Each bluebell emerges from a small, white, hairless bulb. First, in March, the sets of glossy, arrow-shaped leaves with hooded tips spring from the soil. The single flower spike then rises.

From this the delicate, cylindrical bells in hues of white, pink and blue descend in a line, along a graceful curve, in April or May. As bluebells reproduce slowly, by multiplying their bulbs, they are, like wood anemones, indicators of ancient woodland.

Left: In our deciduous woodland, great swathes of bluebells form magical scented seas that flow and ebb on the breeze. Above: The delicate, cylindrical blue bells, which hang down in a line, along a graceful curve, appear in April and May.

'the different shades of blue can appear to shimmer in the right light, as if the flowers are somehow evaporating into the atmosphere'

When bluebells grow in great swaths, the different shades of blue can appear to shimmer in the right light, as if the flowers are somehow evaporating into the atmosphere. The perfume is wonderful too. To inhale the bouquet of other species like primroses and violets, you have to get down on the ground, next to them. With bluebells, however, the heady scent can hit you before you even walk upon the magic carpet. Catch them at their perfumed peak, in a sea of thousands, and the wafting aroma can knock you off your feet.

Places to see – and smell – bluebells abound on National Trust sites. You can get your hit at Hatchlands Park or Winkworth Arboretum, both in Surrey, under the beech avenues at Hinton Ampner in Hampshire, at Sissinghurst Castle Garden in Kent, at Abermawr on the Pembrokeshire coast, at Godolphin or Lanhydrock in Cornwall, under the oaks at Roseberry Topping in North Yorkshire, at Clent Hills in Worcestershire, and in the woods beyond the dunes above the glorious beach at Embleton in Northumberland, to list just a handful of the best locations.

Left: Fresh, green leaves on the trees blend beautifully with bluebells in an ancient woodland at Speke Hall, on the banks of the River Mersey, near Liverpool. Millions of bluebell bulbs may exist in a single wood, creating great carpets of flowers.

If I ever find myself yearning for a quick fix of bluebells in April, I head to Coed-y-Bwnydd. At the end of a long, heavily wooded escarpment above the River Usk, with great views west to the Black Mountains, it is a small but perfectly formed National Trust site in Monmouthshire. The Celtic tribe, the Silures chose this spot for a hill fort some 2,500 years ago. Three concentric earth mounds, the remains of the ramparts, dominate the promontory today. The steep-sided banks to the south and west are covered in thick wood. On the summit, the oaks and the beech are spread out regally among the archaeological ruins allowing plenty of sunlight through.

Coed-y-Bwnydd is a great spot for a walk or a picnic at any time of the year. In spring, though, it is steeped in an irresistible magic. Primroses, a few orchids and in early summer, red campion, all show here, but it is the carpet of bluebells that scores itself into the memory. Hardly an inch of the ancient fort is left uncovered by the mauve flowers. It is an Arcadian vision, an intimation of the beauty and the bounty of nature that existed when the world was young.

Native bluebells are not to be confused with Spanish bluebells, an introduced species planted in gardens and now increasingly common in the wild. Spanish bluebells – stockier with less delicate, paler blue flowers and no scent – cross-breed with native bluebells. The hybrid variety is causing great botanical anxiety – it makes media headlines every spring – because it is now encroaching into our woodlands, watering down the genetics of the native species.

This page: Rods of sunlight illuminate mauve pools on the Blickling Estate, Norfolk. The UK has more bluebells than any other nation, so no wonder they are close to our hearts.

The great flush of bluebells may be the high point of the woodland wild-flower show for many of us, but it is far from the end: wood avens (herb Bennet) is initially hard to spot but once you have identified it, you will see it again and again, and there is wood-sorrel (white, lilac-veined petals and edible leaves that fold up when it gets dark or it rains), foxgloves, lords-and-ladies and red campion among many others, as well as a host of elegant ferns that all appear after the bluebells, when the leaf canopy in the trees has closed over.

Towards the end of spring, several species of woodland flora move to the rides or wide paths that would once have routed working vehicles through the woods, and which are now frequently kept open for conservation purposes.

Left: Red campion is one of many wild flowers that only appear as the bluebells fade, once the leaf canopy in the trees has formed. Above: At the end of spring, several species of flora like foxgloves grow on woodland rides. The tube-shaped pink flowers around a tall stem are magnificent and unmistakable.

M any of our well-known wild-flower species only appear in large numbers when an area of woodland has been recently coppiced. Coppicing is the hugely important and historic woodland practice of cutting broad-leaved trees back to just above ground level to stimulate regrowth from the live stump. Coppicing has been carried out as a form of 'rotation' woodland management for millennia. Certainly, the Celts were managing woodlands productively in this way when the Romans arrived in the first

century AD, though the practice goes back further than that. Boundary banks and ditches, built to keep livestock from grazing on the young growth from cut stumps – many of which are still evident in ancient woodlands across Britain today – illustrate the socio-economic importance of coppice woodland in the Middle Ages. Wood was, until at least the end of the eighteenth century, the most vital natural resource after food – for the construction of ships, as a building material, for fuel and a multitude of other uses.

Above: Coppice woodland at Hatfield Forest, Essex. Coppicing, an ancient form of woodland management that involves cutting broad-leaved trees back to near ground level to stimulate regrowth from the live stump, lets sunlight onto the woodland floor, which stirs a rich diversity of flora into life.

Since the introduction of sweet chestnut by the Romans, this and hazel have been two of the key coppice species in England. They were cut on eight- to 25-year rotations, to yield crops of poles for diverse uses from beanpoles and thatching spars to hop poles and palings. Alder, sycamore, beech, hornbeam, ash and oak all coppice well, and they too were employed extensively in all manner of industries. Coppiced ash, for example, has been used in the manufacture of tool handles, ladders, tent pegs, boat tillers, looms, bobbins, clothes props, crutches, scantlings for stretchers, umbrella handles, walking sticks, catapults, ploughs, cart shafts and axles, harrows, chairs, lobster pots, toboggans, tennis rackets, cricket stumps, oars and bicycle frames, to list just a tiny number of the products traditionally made from it.

This page: From our earliest history until the end of the eighteenth century, wood was a vital natural resource – for building materials, fuel, tool handles and a multitude of other uses. Much of the wood we used came from coppice woodland.

Changes in society, particularly during the Victorian era, the emergence of new sources of fuel, and then the invention of man-made materials like plastic and carbon fibre, led to a massive reduction in the demand for coppice-wood products. Over the course of the twentieth century, many woodlands inevitably fell into neglect; the coppice trees continued to grow, however – they became 'overstood' in silvicultural parlance. More recently, we have come to understand that the practice of coppicing is ecologically very important. When you cut trees back to near ground level, you let sunlight reach the woodland floor for several years, which stirs a rich diversity of flora into life; this, in turn, attracts the insects (notably butterflies) and the birds. The decline in coppicing as a management practice has impacted heavily on the biodiversity of our woodlands. According to the UK conservation organisation, Plantlife, one in six of our woodland flowers is currently threatened with extinction.

Above: Pearl-bordered fritillarys, once widespread, are now seriously threatened. The factors responsible for the general decline in butterfly numbers are not fully understood, but a decline in coppicing – and loss of ancient woodland habitat – have contributed significantly.
Right: Coppice woodland at Hatfield Forest, Essex.
Next page: A formidable, dynamically structured oak tree, coming into leaf in May.

In the woodland I help manage as part of a community group, the rush of winter activities, to coppice the ash and hazel, is over by the beginning of March. There is still plenty to do, of course: the trunks and thicker branches that will be sold locally as firewood need to be cut to length, split and stored under cover to season. The smaller branches will be stacked in the woodland, to be made into barbecue charcoal over the spring and summer.

We stop coppicing and felling trees at the end of winter for two reasons: because the birds are about to begin nesting in the branches, and because the sap in the trees is starting to rise. Sap is the blood of trees. The fluid, comprising mainly water plus a few dissolved minerals, is taken up by a tree's roots from the soil, and transported in a mass of open, tubular vessels that form end to end through the tree like pipelines, to the leaves. Much of the water is then evaporated through the pores of the leaves (called stoma), in a process called transpiration.

These tubular vessels, called xylem, are one of two main kinds of tissues that dominate the structure of all hardwood trees. The other is called phloem (the inner bark), which comprises strings of vascular tissues that carry sugars and other metabolic products of photosynthesis downward from the leaves to all parts of the tree and the associated fungi in the soil.

Between the xylem and the phloem is a thin layer that forms a sheath round the tree, called cambium – a stem-cell tissue that generates more xylem vessels inside it and more phloem on the outside, each year. Thus a tree thickens as it grows older – a process called 'secondary thickening'. The cells that form the tubes of the xylem, in turn, die: all that is left is the cell wall, comprising cellulose (a carbohydrate that forms the cell walls of all plants) stiffened with lignin (a complex organic substance that binds the cellulose and makes it rigid). As successive new layers of xylem are formed, the old xylem becomes increasingly blocked, and solid. It eventually forms the 'heartwood', the part of the tree that holds the whole thing upright.

Left: Piles of coppiced logs in spring: hazel and sweet chestnut were traditionally the two key coppice species in England.
Above: Much coppicing and felling is halted at the end of winter to allow birds like this great spotted woodpecker to begin nesting in the trunks and branches.

Under normal conditions, one new layer of wood is formed around a tree each year. When you look at the cross-section of a tree cut horizontally – the stump of a felled tree or a round of firewood ready for splitting – each new layer appears as a ring. These are commonly referred to as 'growth rings' or 'annual rings', and as any child will tell you, if you count the number of rings, you have the age of the tree. These concentric rings vary in width from species to species; they also vary in width within an individual tree, according to the growing

conditions of the particular year. In Britain the growing season is March to October.

Trees produce new cells each year to perform two main functions: to support the crown of the tree, so it can maintain its position above shorter plants in order to capture more sunlight, enabling photosynthesis to take place in the leaves; and to transport the sap from the soil to the leaves. The cell walls provide the mechanical support for the tree, while the water and nutrients are transported in the cell cavities. Since both the mechanical support and the transportation functions are required in the longitudinal axis of the tree –

upwards – most of the cells that form the xylem are oriented in that direction. Thus, if you magnify the cross-section of a tree, it is a bit like looking end on at a huge bunch of straws.

In some species such as oak, chestnut and ash, the cells are relatively large and distinct: in some cases, they may be seen with the naked eye. In other species, the cells can only be identified with a magnifying glass. Where there is a visible contrast within a single growth ring (as with ash), the inner or first formed layer of xylem is called 'earlywood' (or sometimes 'springwood'), and the outer layer of xylem is called 'latewood' (or

'summerwood'). The earlywood forms during the first part of the annual growing season, when growth is rapid: it comprises thin-walled, lower density cells or vessels with larger cavities that appear lighter in colour. The latewood cells, created towards the end of the growing cycle, are smaller, thicker-walled, denser and darker. Latewood also contains a greater proportion of lignin and other wood fibres that give strength and toughness to wood.

This page: Sunlight pours into woodland at Leith Hill, Surrey, lighting up the new growth.

As the last memories of winter retreat from the woods, the dawn chorus of birdsong – nature's original alarm clock – reaches its annual peak, usually around the first week of May. This avian euphoria can be heard earlier in the year – February, for example, is a good month to listen out for native bird song – but by May all the migrant species have arrived and the volume is turned up to maximum. You do have to be up very early, with the lark as the old saying goes, to hear the opening volleys of the chorus. The roll call begins about an hour before sunrise, though the exact time depends on where you are in the country: between the vernal and autumnal equinoxes, the sun rises earlier in the north than in the south of the UK. In early May, 4 a.m. is a good guideline for the South of England.

Insect eaters and birds with large eyes are commonly the first to clear their throats. In the woodlands, there is some regularity to the sequence: often, the blackbird begins, then the song thrush, pheasant, wood pigeon, robin, garden warbler, black cap, mistle thrush, willow warbler, wren, great tit, chiffchaff, great spotted woodpecker, chaffinch, nuthatch and treecreeper. Personally, I struggle to distinguish between the individual songs, particularly when the cacophony really gets going, but I am told it is possible, if you can summon the powers of concentration to follow just one song at a time.

The chorus line-up comprises male songbirds. They are singing first and foremost to attract a mate, but also to mark out their breeding territory and then, later in spring, to defend it. As soon as it is light enough to look for food, the chorus starts to tail off, as the hungry birds get busy. There is a dusk chorus too, but these urgent calls to love and war are loudest and sweetest at dawn, as it tends to be less windy then, and sound travels better. Aside from the dawn chorus, early May is an excellent time of year for birdwatching in general. All through the day, woodlands are full of movement, alarm calls, the thrum of wings and the drumming of woodpeckers. Because there are still only a few leaves on the trees, you can often spot the birds zipping through the branches or sitting on a twig perch.

The song of the wild (clockwise from top left): the much-admired songster, the nightingale; the song thrush, another diva; the softly spoken wood warbler and the throaty cuckoo.

May is an inspirational time to be in woodland for many reasons. I have read that it is the moment in the year when British expatriates ache for home the most. All the senses are sated: while the birds are in song, the scent of wild flowers rises from the floor. The shapes of the branches are still just about visible, while many are newly decorated with buds and then with bright new leaves. If you are quick, you can even eat some of the leaves: beech (a bit lemony) and hawthorn (nutty) are both edible. They are both best in salads, but you have to pick them before they have seen too much sun and become bitter.

The sense of touch can be enlivened too, by running your hands over the bark of different trees when they are full of vigorous growth in spring. Beech bark, smooth with feint horizontal impressions, feels like sun-dried rind. Holly bark – lightly roughened with small, round widely spaced warts – is also distinctive. With your eyes closed, it is hard to distinguish between wild cherry – rough, lenticel-bands and horizontal strips of peeling paper-bark – and downy birch – sharp, vertical patterning and similar rolls of flaking paper. This is strange, when you consider how clearly distinguishable the two trees are by sight. The bark of ash trees is harder to recognise by touch.

Young ash trees have smooth bark but as they age, it cracks to form a pattern of fluted ridges and vertical fissures, like the impressions left by waves in the sand on a beach. Oak bark is similarly ridged, but the raised bands are often short, deeper, knobbly and irregular. My favourite tree by touch is field maple: the bark is closely ridged, even when the trees are young, and slightly corky. Field maple bark also feels warm in cold weather.

In the midst of this sensory overload, we fail to observe the emergence of summer in the same fastidious detail as we do the coming of spring. Summer is a season that tends to creep up on us, but if you are a regular visitor to woodland in May, the signs are all there. The leaf canopy slowly closes and the air among the trees grows heavier. Many of the colourful wild flowers bow out. Even the creamy-white flowers on the ubiquitous, superlative hawthorn tree – for centuries a symbol of fertility and rebirth – that breathe life into the countryside in April, now fade. Sometimes, the climax of spring feels terminal. Actually, it is just a new beginning.

Left and above: Rough bark on an ancient oak tree at Whiddon Deer Park, on the north-eastern edge of Dartmoor, Devon. The bark of old oaks is fissured and ridged with short, deep, knobbly and irregular raised bands.

SUMMER

'Let the forest be judge'
___

As You Like It, William Shakespeare

Toys Hill, near Sevenoaks in Kent, includes 450 acres (182ha) of mainly ancient woodland and heath. This National Trust property lies across Greensand Ridge, an escarpment bordering the Weald, the once heavily wooded strip of England that stretches between the parallel chalk uplands of the North and the South Downs. 'Weald' is an Old English word for 'forest'; the area still has an abundance of woodlands today.

Octavia Hill, a formidable social reformer and one of the co-founders of the National Trust in 1895, grew up near here. In 1898, Hill gave the nascent organisation one of its first properties – the terrace and the well on the south side of the escarpment, in the hamlet of Toys Hill. The donation was part of an initiative to protect green spaces in and around London, and open them up to the general public. That people should have free access to common land, including woodlands, was a radical idea at the end of the Victorian era. Since then, the National Trust has steadily acquired a large stretch of the wooded sandstone ridge above the hamlet.

Left: Dawn view from Toys Hill, one of the highest points in Kent, looking south over the Weald. The area was one of the first properties to be donated to the National Trust in 1898.

For centuries, these ancient woodlands were gently sculpted by man: charcoal burners, herdsmen grazing pigs, road builders quarrying chert stone, artisans extracting timber and local villagers gathering firewood have all left their mark. More recently, the woodlands were dramatically refashioned by wind. Toys Hill was at the epicentre of the Great Storm of October 1987. Some 95 per cent of the mature oak and beech trees along the top of the escarpment were flattened during that momentous night. In the aftermath, photographs of Greensand Ridge showed a level of destruction that was hard to comprehend: from the air, the scene was like a *trompe-l'oeil* – of splintered matches scattered on a basket of dried moss.

Almost 30 years later, in the breathless vortex of high summer, I set off on foot across the ridge at Toys Hill. It was a July morning during a heatwave. The sticks crackled and snapped under my boots. Woodpigeons were cooing lazily. Partly because of public pressure, the worst affected tracts of woodland were machine-cleared of all the fallen tree debris after the storm – the fires burnt for months – and then replanted, mainly with oak and beech.

This page: An aerial view of the woodlands at Toys Hill following the Great Storm of 15 and 16 October 1987. Some 95 per cent of the mature oak and beech trees on the escarpment at Toys Hill were flattened.

Unfortunately, birch has since extensively colonised these areas, shading out most of the trees that were planted. Walking from the car park up to the site of the old manor house at Weardale, almost every tree I passed was birch. There are a few oaks and the odd beech which pre-date 1987, but for the most part, this formerly rich and varied ancient woodland is now a birch monoculture. Walking through it quickly became monotonous.

In one of the woodlands at Toys Hill, however, the National Trust managed to resist the pressure and the urge to clean up after the Great Storm. Scords Wood, which I had come to visit, is an 80 acre (32.4ha) area that was simply left alone when the winds abated in October 1987. Many of the trees here are upended and dead: their moss-covered stumps and great, rotting trunks now look like an outlandish set from a children's fantasy film. An equal number of the trees carried on growing after the storm, though, albeit at strange angles and in unlikely directions.

This page: An aerial photograph of woodland at Toys Hill taken in 2007, twenty years after the Great Storm. In the areas that were machine-cleared and replanted in 1987, birch has outgrown almost everything else, to create a monoculture.
Right: Scords Wood, an 80 acre (32.4ha) site at Toys Hill that was left untouched after the Great Storm. Today, it feels more like the remains of a primeval forest in Eastern Europe than a wood in Kent.

'The tangle of roots and boughs reflects the battles that have taken place to gain pieces of sky since 1987'

Today, many of the live, horizontal trunks have sent new branches vertically upwards. The tangle of roots and boughs reflects the battles that have taken place to gain pieces of sky since 1987. Wild strawberries, wood avens and ragwort, among other unusual species of flora, are now flourishing in the holes left by uprooted trees and on the exposed root plates. This 'pit and mound' ecosystem is more characteristic of the remains of primeval forests in Eastern Europe and North America than Kent woodland. Ecologists have found interesting fungi and rare invertebrate species here. The shape, the lines, the way the light falls irregularly through the canopy and the whole structure of Scords Wood is alien, and enchanting.

After the storm (clockwise from top left): Wild flowers like wild strawberries and wood avens thrive in sunny glades while fungi take advantage of fallen trees. Insects, like this red admiral, feast on the bounty.

I ventured off the sunken path that bisects the wood. Almost immediately, I was on my hands and knees, ducking under fractured branches and rolling over decaying trunks. I almost fell headlong into a hole created by an upended oak and I limboed under the arms of a prostrate beech pollard. There were trees collapsed against their neighbours, in a form of arboreal embrace. In places, the air was stifled with the must of rotting wood and teeming with clusters of insects; elsewhere, sunlight fell in wide pools of dappled gold. I had to weave through hornbeam and ash saplings sprouting out of rotting debris. Occasionally, I came across a root ball on its side, a great half moon of desiccated earth and gnarled roots woven back and forth into one another like the threads of a Celtic knot. At times, I simply couldn't penetrate any further in one direction, so I turned around and tried another. Soon enough, I lost all sense of where I was.

It is plausible that the original 'wildwood' – the natural woodland that covered large parts of Britain, and all of the Weald, before the beginning of large-scale human activity, some time in the Neolithic period – was full of supine, living trees, great lumps of decaying wood and a rich diversity of ground flora, like Scords Wood.

Previous page: A carpet of ferns covers the woodland floor on the Stackpole Estate, Pembrokeshire: woodland ferns are shade tolerant, which means they can prosper throughout summer when the trees are in leaf.
Left: Exposed root plate of a fallen oak tree.
Above: A garden woodlouse, the most common of the 35 species of woodlice native to the UK, survives on a diet of rotting wood.

Certainly, the policy of hands-off management, or 'non-intervention' in forestry parlance, after the 1987 storm has proved to be a boon for nature here. The vigorous, natural rejuvenation has prompted foresters and woodland owners, including the National Trust, to reappraise the adaptability of ancient woodlands. The species diversity in Scords Wood contrasts dramatically with the monoculture birch woodlands that were machine-cleared and replanted after the Great Storm. When hurricane-force winds next hit southern Britain, we will manage our woodlands very differently in the aftermath.

By the time I found a path that led me out of Scords Wood, the sun was high in the sky. I walked past a bed of bright yellow marsh-marigolds and, nearby, a patch of hazy pink ragged-robins. At 770ft (235m) above sea level, Greensand Ridge rises over most of Kent. From the hamlet of Toys Hill there are panoramic views over the expanse of the Weald. Plump, brilliant-white clouds dotted the sky all the way to the horizon. I thought of Sir Winston Churchill, who lived nearby at Chartwell for 40 years. Looking out on a similar aspect, he once declared: 'This is what we're fighting for.'

Left: The delicate pink flowers of ragged-robin bloom in summer on open rides, particularly in damp woods.
Below: View from the terrace at Chartwell in Kent, home of Winston Churchill for 40 years, looking south over the great wooded expanse of the Weald.

There are only 59 species of butterfly on these islands, and many of them are rare. Yet, among the 20,000 or so species of insects found in the UK, butterflies have an enduring hold on the human imagination. Their importance is reflected in how they represent many different things to different people: to an ecologist, butterflies are indicators of a healthy ecosystem; to a child, a butterfly flying from a leaf and rising through a column of sunlight in a woodland glade can be a moment of rapture; to all of us, butterflies are an abiding symbol of summer.

In fact, some species of woodland butterflies first appear in spring. You might catch sight of a lemon-coloured brimstone with its leaf-shaped wings, sunbathing on ivy in early April. Orange tips, so distinctive in flight and yet brilliantly camouflaged at rest, are widely distributed across the UK; they also appear in spring, in meadows, gardens and woodlands. These species are merely warm-up acts, though – advanced publicity for the main butterfly performance that begins with genuine gusto in June.

Left: On a beautiful summer day, take a blanket to the woods and lie down on your back under the canopies of different trees, to admire them from a new angle.

Above: Brimstone butterfly with lemon-coloured wings, nectaring on red campion.

'to all of us, butterflies are an abiding symbol of summer'

One of the few species of butterfly you will see only in the woodlands is the white admiral. With black wings illuminated by a white band, it is unmistakable. The caterpillars hatch on honeysuckle leaves before metamorphosing in June. The adult butterflies then feed and bask in sunny glades, flitting from flower to flower with minimum effort and great delicacy, through to the end of July.

The speckled wood – cocoa-brown with creamy spots – similarly appears in puddles of light in the heart of woodlands, from mid-summer to September, as does the ringlet. With velvety, dark-coloured wings and lighter trim, ringlets are relatively common all over the UK. Occasionally they appear *en masse*, in large woodland clearings. At the other end of the scale is the elusive purple emperor. Large, with iridescent purple wings lit by a white band, this is one of our rarest butterflies. The best chance of spotting one on the wing is at the beginning or end of a hot day from July to August, when they descend from the canopy of broad-leaved trees to feed on the woodland floor. Once common across a much larger area, the habitat of the purple emperor has shrunk in recent decades, to sites in central southern England. The black hairstreak is even more confined in its distribution. Notoriously difficult to identify, this elusive species has also declined steadily over the last century. The few remaining colonies breed in thickets of mature blackthorn, in sunny, sheltered parts of woodlands on clay soils across a narrow belt of the East Midlands.

A kaleidoscope of butterflies (clockwise from top left): The elusive and strikingly beautiful purple emperor, one of our rarest butterflies; a speckled wood butterfly; a black hairstreak, now limited to the east Midlands and a ringlet – these occasionally appear *en masse*, in large woodland clearings.

The factors responsible for the decline in butterfly numbers are not fully understood, but it is thought that changes in woodland management practices – more specifically, the decline in coppicing – and the loss of ancient woodland habitat, have contributed significantly. Many butterfly species thrive on the combination of mature trees and ground flora that woodland clearings, glades and open rides in actively managed, multi-aged, broad-leaved woodlands happen to provide. Not all species are in decline, though. A minority, including white admirals (which are shade tolerant) and ringlets, have fared better over the last half century.

The National Trust has done much to adapt woodland management practices in order to improve and increase habitat for butterflies. In fact, several properties have become renowned for spotting these captivating insects. At Bookham Common in Surrey, for example, you have a chance of seeing a purple emperor in mid-July.

Over 40 species inhabit the chalk grasslands and the beautiful ancient woodlands on Box Hill, also in Surrey. The 149 acres (60.3ha) of mixed woodlands at Arnside Knott in Cumbria are home to high brown fritillaries (rare) and Scotch argus (extremely rare in England). At Ashclyst Forest on the Killerton Estate in Devon, the woods are explicitly managed for some of our rarer species, such as pearl-bordered fritillaries. Common and widespread only a generation ago, this butterfly is now seriously threatened. In Ashclyst Forest, you might also catch a glimpse of dark green fritillaries, purple emperors and silver-washed fritillaries, as well as several of the more common species, including ringlets, common blues, speckled woods and marbled whites.

This page: In certain locations, the National Trust is working to adapt woodland management practices to improve habitat for butterflies. On the Killerton Estate in Devon, pictured here, the woods are managed for rare species like pearl-bordered fritillaries.

On Selborne Common in Hampshire, you can admire butterflies while walking in the footsteps of pioneering naturalist, the Reverend Gilbert White. His letters to friends detailing his observations on nature in his immediate locality were published in 1789 as *The Natural History of Selborne*. This *tour de force* of nature writing has been in print ever since. In the emerald shade of the beech trees that White knew so well, and under the glades of ash on the chalk common, you might be lucky enough to spot brown hairstreaks, purple emperors and silver-washed fritillaries. Watching a silver-washed fritillary – a large butterfly with orange and black upper wings – flit and swoop across a sun-soaked oak glade is a mesmerising experience. As White understood, though, you cannot simply

pre-order encounters like this. Spotting butterflies – brightly decorated intimations of the beauty, the bounty and the perpetual youth that is bound up in our woodlands – takes time. You have to return to the glades again and again, to sit and silently observe the summer unfold. You have to visit with alternative motives. As Louis MacNeice wrote, you have to come to the woods to set your 'mind adrift in a floating, rustling ark' and hope you get lucky.

Left: Purple emperor larva. This rare species occurs in large woodlands where goat willow, the primary larva foodplant, is abundant.

Above: If you are lucky, you might spot a brown hairstreak on Selborne Common, Hampshire, where Gilbert White lived and wrote *The Natural History of Selborne*.

Many birds stop singing when they start to moult into a new set of feathers, in the middle of summer. Nightingales, celebrated over centuries for their dulcet song that fills the woods in April and May, are silent by mid-June. Cuckoos, also summer visitors but more widely dispersed than nightingales, cease their distinctive song in early to mid-June, and then often disappear. Even the woodlark, whose melodious, liquid trill enlivens wood pasture and heathland throughout southern and eastern England in spring, and which inspired both Gerard Manley Hopkins and Robert Burns to poetry, is mute by the beginning of July. In fact, because so many birds are suddenly inaudible, July used to be known as the 'silent month' in Britain.

Above: The 'sweet warbling woodlark' that inspired Robert Burns to poetry.
Right: In high summer, the birds are still busy in places like Adkin's Wood, in the grounds of Ickworth House, Suffolk – you just have to stop and listen more carefully to hear them.
Next page: The high forest of mainly beech, oak and ash in Aston Wood, on the Chilterns escarpment in eastern Oxfordshire, is glorious on a July evening.

At this time of year, the woodlands are actually still busy with bird life: you just have to listen more carefully. On a sultry afternoon, you might hear a woodpigeon cooing in the canopy – the gentlest of all territorial avian songs – or a red kite mewing above the trees. On another day, hungry green woodpecker chicks will be calling noisily for their parents, from a nest inside the trunk of a dead or dying tree. Occasionally, a large flock – or 'murder' – of crows will make a din as they gather on a woodland edge. If you are prepared to wait patiently among fruiting wild cherry and hawthorn trees, you might even catch a flock of secretive hawfinches on a family feeding foray, before they return to dense woodland to roost. Towards the end of summer, many species of migratory birds, including willow warblers, wood warblers and pied flycatchers, begin fattening themselves up and gathering boisterously, in preparation for the journey south.

Left: On a sultry, summer afternoon in the woods, listen for a red kite mewing above the trees.
Above: Migratory birds like willow warblers (pictured here, perched on hawthorn), start fattening up and then gathering in gangs towards the end of summer, before migrating south to sub-Saharan Africa.

'their beauty is ephemeral: strong winds and squalls of rain can scatter the petals along woodland rides like confetti'

As well as being a favourite of the birds, wild cherry is one of our loveliest native woodland trees. Though widely distributed across the country, it tends to grow in drifts through mixed, broad-leaved stands. Often, you have to look for it. In spring, wild cherry produces intense displays of white flowers, which can stop you in your tracks on a walk. These clusters of cup-shaped flowers provide an early source of nectar and pollen for bees, but their beauty is ephemeral: strong winds and squalls of rain can scatter the petals along woodland rides like confetti, soon after they appear.

Come summer, wild cherry trees realise a more permanent splendour. The bark of mature trees has a purple-brown hue and cream-coloured, horizontal bands. The leaves are long and oval shaped, with coarse teeth and pointed tips. The black and crimson fruits attract blackbirds, song thrushes and hawfinches, among others, from mid-July. When these cherries fall from the trees, badgers, dormice and wood mice gorge on them.

Cherry pickers (clockwise from top left): Song thrushes visit the woods in July to feast on wild cherries while dormice wait until the fruits fall to the woodland floor before gorging; a young badger forages in the sunshine and a hawfinch roosts in dense woodland.

W e, too, have eaten cherries for millennia. From Tudor times until the middle of the twentieth century, cherry trees were cultivated in orchards, notably in Kent, for the fruit, which was used extensively in cooking and medicine. Wild cherry wood was in common usage too, for joinery, turning and musical instruments. Timber from the best trees is a rich, reddish brown colour and highly prized by cabinetmakers.

The contrast between the bark, the green leaves and the fruit in wild cherry trees is always worth admiring. You do have to stop and look up though, as the cherries will be high in the canopy of this fast-growing tree. Even better, take a blanket to the woods on a summer's day and lie down under the canopies of different species, to admire them from a new angle.

Sweet or Spanish chestnuts are also good to eat. The long, elegant leaves are loosely assembled and hang at an angle. Because of their size, the shape of each one can be picked out in the gossamer light under the boughs. If you find an old sweet chestnut to lie under, admire how the stretched out vertical fissures in the bark form a spiral (usually clockwise) up the trunk.

Left: Sweet chestnut trees have been widely cultivated, for the edible nuts and for the excellent wood, over millennia. The bark on old trees tends to spiral clockwise.

Next page: Sycamore trees will grow almost anywhere.

The sycamore tree is equally lavish in its summer decoration. The leaves are five-lobed, open-handed and ever-so-slightly human in form.

We have a strange relationship with the sycamore tree in Britain. In many ways, it is a benevolent species: the clumps of dark green leaves afford deep shade – welcome relief if you are working hard in the woods in August; the sticky sap attracts a horde of aphids in summer, which in turn provides a café in the canopy for many bird species; the tree is both remarkably adept at self-regenerating and quick to fill gaps in woodlands (though it rarely dominates them); sycamores will grow almost anywhere, and they grow fast; the wood from sycamores is attractive, clean, inexpensive and easy to work, at least compared to oak. There is hardly a downside to the tree, yet it remains unloved. It is curious. The fact that the species is so common – and self-seeds so vigorously, to the ire of gardeners – may stir in us a sense of silvicultural snobbery, which we struggle to shift. Also, the sycamore was introduced to Britain, probably in the fifteenth century. It is a non-native species, and that stands as a mark against it for some.

Another non-native species, the grey squirrel, is doing what it can to restrict the regeneration of sycamores. Grey squirrels were introduced in 1876 – the innocent act of Thomas Brocklehurst, a prosperous financier who brought a pair back from a trip to North America and let them loose in the grounds of his Cheshire home. He cannot have imagined how they would thrive. The population of grey squirrels in Britain is now estimated at three million. Their advance across the country has been at the expense of native red squirrels, which are smaller, breed more slowly and succumb to a lethal disease carried by the greys. The population of red squirrels – around 160,000 – is now confined to woodlands in Scotland, the North of England and Northern Ireland, with small numbers in Wales and some islands off the south coast, including the Isle of Wight and Brownsea Island, Dorset. In many places, the reds rely extensively on expensive conservation initiatives.

Grey squirrels have adapted remarkably well to urban environments and are common in city parks and gardens. For many of us, seeing a grey squirrel is one of the few recurrent wildlife encounters we have. However, grey squirrels are public enemy number one in woodlands. Aside from the impact they have on native red squirrels, greys do untold damage to broad-leaved trees. They strip the bark, which can have serious consequences for the health of a tree. If just one area of bark is stripped, it leaves a scar making the tree vulnerable to pests and diseases. However, if bark is stripped the entire way round a trunk – a process called 'ring barking' – that tree will die. As well as sycamore, the species grey squirrels preferentially attack include field maple, oak, silver birch and beech. Young trees aged ten to 40 years old are particularly susceptible. In some instances, the impact of grey squirrels is stifling natural regeneration in ancient woodlands.

The economic and environmental impact of squirrel damage is now widely recognised in the world of woodland management and tree cultivation. The National Trust is part of a recent initiative to control grey squirrels. The UK Squirrel Accord, supported by over 30 conservation, woodland management, timber industry and landowning organisations, aims to promote a new coordinated strategy, which will reduce the impact of grey squirrels on woodlands, and hopefully secure the future of the reds too.

Right: Grey squirrels now thrive in Britain, at the expense of native red squirrels. Grey squirrels do untold damage to broad-leaved trees, attracting the ire of woodland owners and foresters.

Ash is my favourite tree to lie under. In woodlands, ash forms a trunk free of side branches, which offers a clean view from below, up the mast-straight stem and into the well-proportioned canopy. The compound, pinnate (from the Latin word *pinnatus* meaning 'feathered') leaves comprise pairs of leaflets placed opposite each other on a central stalk, usually with a single leaflet at the end. The leaflets are lance-shaped, slender-pointed, tapered at both ends and 2–5in (5–12.7cm) long with toothed edges. They are dark green, smooth on top and paler underneath. Occasionally, the end leaflet is absent. The relative rarity of this led to the once-popular belief that an ash leaf with an even number of leaflets would bring good luck: 'Even ash I do thee pluck, / Hoping thus to meet good luck, / If no good luck I get from thee, / I shall wish thee on the tree,' is an old English rhyme.

In the Middle Ages, young girls in the north of England hoping to meet a husband at a fair would traditionally pluck even ash leaves and place them in their left shoe.

In high summer, when the year stands still, ash leaves are first to receive the impression of a breeze, hissing softly as if they are fanning the sky. Gerard Manley Hopkins described ash leaves as 'painted on air'. Lie on your back in an ash grove and the experience is faintly psychedelic. A soft, translucent light leaks freely through the myriad divisions between the feathery leaflets.

Ash is currently infected by the disease known as 'ash dieback', and summer happens to be a good time of year to look for the symptoms. Also known as Chalara, the disease was first observed in the UK in 2012. It has since spread to many sites throughout the British Isles, though the east and south-east remain the most seriously

infected areas. The symptoms of ash dieback – wilted leaves, dark strips of bark on twigs, diamond-shaped lesions on stems with dead twigs or branches in the middle and new growth from buds below the infected part – can be hard to diagnose, particularly in spring and autumn. They are most evident in young trees or coppice shoots, which are more readily affected than older trees, and this is where to start a survey.

In large ash trees, the process from initial infection to death can take several years, while some trees infected with Chalara don't seem to die: genetic factors mean they have a tolerance of or even a resistance to the disease – a cause for some hope.

Ash dieback was first observed in Europe around 1990, in Poland and the Baltic states of Latvia and Lithuania. Its rapid spread to most parts of the Continent has been substantially aided by man, with disastrous effect. The disease is caused by a microscopic fungus, *Hymenoscyphus fraxineus*, which inhabits ash leaves and twigs. In summer, the fungus produces a chemical, which is toxic to the tree. From summer through to autumn, it produces dust-like spores from infected dead leaves, which spread very efficiently – mainly on the wind but also on our boots and coats. No one is certain how, or even if the fungus was first introduced to Europe: it might be a mutation or hybridisation of a previously existing fungus, or it may have been inadvertently imported from Asia, where the fungus is known: it has co-evolved with species of ash in Korea and Japan over a long period of time and does them no harm.

Above: Ash leaves comprise lance-shaped leaflets in pairs, usually with a single leaflet at the end of the stalk. Leaves with an even number of leaflets were once thought to bring good luck.

There is another, even greater threat to our ash trees, though fortunately it has not yet reached the UK. The emerald ash borer, a voracious and destructive beetle, also originally from Asia, was introduced by mistake to the USA in the 1990s. Most likely, it arrived in wooden packing material used to transport goods. It has since killed tens of millions of ash trees across North America. The metallic-green beetle can only travel short distances each year but its spread has been maximised by the movement of ash nursery stock, timber, wood chip and firewood. In fact, human behaviour has been a defining factor in the impact of the emerald ash borer.

Various multi-disciplinary teams of scientists from government agencies and universities have devised several ways to stem the impairment of America's ash trees. Such initiatives are all focused on slowing the spread: eradication of the emerald ash borer is no longer regarded as feasible, while the cost of trying to control the beetle's impact is already in the hundreds of millions of dollars. The beetle has more recently been identified in Russia, east of Moscow. It seems inevitable that it will reach Western Europe. Predictions are difficult, but it is reasonable to assume that the populations of ash in both Europe and North America, along with a wide array of biodiversity that depends on the species, will continue to be devastated over the next century.

Previous page: The spread of tree pests and pathogens around the world is gathering pace. It is hard to predict how this proliferation will affect our magnificent native woodlands in the future.
Left: Elegant ash tree in full leaf.
Above: The emerald ash borer beetle, originally from Asia, is spreading west and south of Moscow at a rate of 25 miles (41km) per year.

The spread of tree pests and diseases around the world is nothing new. In some instances, it is nature taking its course. However, when international trade increased exponentially in the nineteenth century, plant and tree blights inevitably followed; pests and diseases that had co-evolved with certain host tree species in one place over time, wreaked havoc when they were introduced to new, unadapted hosts in other parts of the world. Around the beginning of the twentieth century, wealthy countries alarmed at the incidence of new pests and diseases impacting trees of significant economic or ecological importance, instituted basic biosecurity regimes at their national borders. The incidence slowed, though efforts prevented neither the fungus, American chestnut blight, from effectively wiping out chestnuts in the USA between the 1900s and 1940, nor Dutch elm disease, transmitted by the elm bark beetle, which wreaked havoc across America, New Zealand and Europe during the second half of the twentieth century.

Above: Dead elm tree near Sherborne, Gloucestershire. Dutch elm disease, caused by a fungus disseminated by the elm bark beetle, killed over 60 million British elms in two epidemics in the twentieth century. It is still spreading today.

Until relatively recently, the incidence of new tree pests and diseases in many developed countries remained linear. Today, the spread of pests and pathogens around the world is gathering pace again, probably as a result of human travel, the escalation of trade and an increase in containerised shipping.

In the UK, there seems to be some new tree blight every few years. London plane trees are affected by a disease called Massaria. Many thousands of acres of larch plantations have been felled across western Britain in the last few years because of infection from the fungus-like pathogen, *Phytophthora ramorum*. Horse chestnut trees are at risk from both a deadly bleeding canker and a leaf mining beetle. Oriental chestnut gall wasp, which affects sweet chestnut trees, was discovered in a UK woodland in 2015. Our oaks are susceptible to the Asian longhorn beetle, the oak processionary moth (of concern with respect to human health and well as tree health) and acute oak decline. Even our ash trees have started succumbing to ash dieback. Until recently, foresters thought ash was going to be the 'tree of the future', but it could so easily become a tree of the past.

To anticipate and protect against new pests and diseases, and to prevent heaping further catastrophe on our trees, we need government action: to invest in improving plant pathology; to introduce stricter plant and soil quarantine regulations on our borders, and to scale up pre-shipping pesticide treatments and biosecurity inspections; and also to prevent the importation of trees, plants and soil in such volume. Perhaps more importantly, we need to learn to value our native trees and woodlands once again.

This page: Let's hope the sight of a blighted tree doesn't become the norm. We need to work together to protect what we have – while we still have it.

'It is not so much for its beauty that the forest makes a claim upon men's hearts, as for that subtle something, that quality of the air, that emanation from the old trees, that so wonderfully changes and renews a weary spirit,' Robert Louis Stevenson wrote in his essay 'Forest Notes' in 1876. Near the end of summer, this feeling is most apparent in woodlands; when the airless vacuum underneath the canopy begins to leak, when the sun-metallic leaves soften, when the drowsiness is disturbed and the trees stop listening, when summer teeters on its irregular apex, then there is a new spirit abroad with the power to affect the weary. In particular, Stevenson's 'subtle something' works like magic on children: our woodlands provide royal playgrounds. We need to remember that appreciating and understanding trees is part of what it means to be human, and we need to take our children to the woods more often. For them, a gathering of trees is not simply a place rich with profitable timber or abundant with nature, but rather it is a hideout full of danger and enchantment. Woodlands are the province of older beliefs, places of lawlessness and havens for the just – children feel this instinctively.

Many of the woodlands owned by the National Trust today have survived the arrival of Neolithic farmers who felled trees to make way for agriculture, the passion of the Norman hegemony for hunting, the first agricultural revolution, the Little Ice Age, the grazing of livestock, supplying timber to the English Navy, the exhaustive demands of the Industrial Revolution, the coming of coal and then oil as domestic heating fuel, the invention of plastic and the idiocy of twentieth-century forestry policy. Somehow through all this, they have remained relevant to successive generations of disparate owners and woodsmen. And now, as extant parts of a forgotten landscape, they have a vital role in our cultural imagination.

This page: Evening sunlight slants through a tree canopy on the Ickworth Estate, Suffolk. The desire to appreciate and understand trees is part of what it means to be human.

AUTUMN

'The lost leaves measure our years'

_____

The Life of the Fields, Richard Jeffries

'there is an ancestral calling at this time of year:
the gathering winds, the reopening of the sky'

Come autumn, the experience of being in the woods is somehow amplified. There is plenty of foraging to be done – for mushrooms to fill the larder and berries to make vitamin-packed jellies. More than this, though, there is an ancestral calling at this time of year: the gathering winds, the reopening of the sky and the dramatic changes that take place as the trees reorganise themselves for winter, all summon us to the woods to witness nature and reflect upon our relationship with it.

In Japan, *Shinrin-yoku* or 'forest bathing' is established as a standard, modern form of preventative medicine, as well as an enjoyable pastime. Essentially, *Shinrin-yoku* involves going for a stroll in a woodland or forest, preferably an old one. You might pause occasionally on this walk, to observe your surroundings closely. *Shinrin-yoku* does not involve running, mountain biking, tree-canopy walks, climbing or any other energetic pursuit. The focus is on slowing down and allowing nature to soak into your body through all five senses.

Left: In autumn, the dramatic changes that take place in trees inspire us to appreciate our place in the natural world.
Above: Waxwings arrive in the UK from mid-autumn, feeding on the fruit of trees like rowan and hawthorn.

The Japanese government only coined the term *Shinrin-yoku* in 1982, though the practice is inspired by an appreciation of our place in the natural world, which was embodied in Shinto and Buddhist practices long ago. Today, nearly a quarter of the Japanese population enjoy forest bathing. Because of its broad popularity, scientists have been able to conduct biological field studies to find out just how spending time strolling among old trees is beneficial to us, at a molecular level, in our cells and neurons.

The research data is compelling. Leisurely walks in the greenwood increase cognition, reduce heart rate and blood pressure, decrease sympathetic nerve activity and lower levels of the stress hormone, cortisol (which in turn makes us less prone to heart disease and depression). It seems our most common physiological responses to spending time among trees are all positive. There is no downside. If you are a regular visitor to the woods, you probably don't need scientists to tell you this, especially in autumn when the leaf colour fireworks are starting to go off.

This page: Hatfield Forest, Essex is the best surviving example in Britain of a medieval hunting forest and home to many different types of woodland, as well as a wealth of ancient pollard trees, including oaks, field maple and famously, hornbeams.

During summer, the cells in leaves are full of the wondrous green pigment chlorophyll, which soaks up sunlight for the alchemical process at the root of all plant life – photosynthesis. Chlorophyll absorbs the blue and red light of the sun, but reflects the green intensely. In autumn, though, the sap that carries water from the soil to the leaves stops flowing, chlorophyll breaks down and green is no longer reflected in the leaf cells. The concentrated, often colourful and distinctive pigments in the leaves of the different species of trees are then vividly revealed. Field maples, for example, contain anthocyanins, which produce a palate of red pigments; oak and willow contain carotenoids, which turn leaves yellow, orange and brown.

We still don't fully understand the reason for all these different pigments in the leaves. It may simply be a reaction to the changing leaf physiology connected to cooling temperatures. Possibly, the pigments allow trees to capitalise on the weakening sun. It has even been suggested that the pigments might serve either to repel or attract insects. Whatever the reason for the different pigments, autumn leaf colour is to be savoured for as long as possible.

The earliest hints of colour in the canopy commonly appear in late September. Horse chestnut trees are increasingly the first to turn because of the spread of a tree pest called the leaf miner moth. Ash leaflets are next and fade to pale yellow; field maple then turns, along with beech and silver birch; hazel and oak are commonly last. By mid-October, with the right weather conditions, all the tree species are turning and the woodlands are ablaze with their tribal dyes.

Seen from afar, woodlands with a good variety of broad-leaved tree species can have canopies that resemble patchwork quilts of orange, yellow, crimson, russet, auburn, copper, tan, tawny, scarlet and gold. On closer inspection, the hues and dyes are inconceivably varied: even two turning leaves from the same tree can differ enormously in detail. Not every year produces the full, vibrant spectrum of colour, though. Ideal conditions include a dry summer, then a spell of bright, sunny autumn days without freezing nights.

The colours of autumn (clockwise from top left): From the crisp green of silver birch leaves to the yellows and reds of acers and the rich browns of the red oak, autumn is a veritable artist's palette.

This page: Delicately coloured beech leaves in woodland at Sheringham Park, on the north Norfolk coast. Humphry Repton famously designed the parkland in 1812: it is surrounded by a rich mix of habitats including heath, cliff top dunes and ancient woodland.

'On a perfectly still day, when the mist steals through the trees
like a thief, I like to stop in the middle of a wood
and look up for a few minutes to watch a single leaf fall'

The peak of colour (or full leaf tint), according to people who study phenology or seasonal natural phenomena, is usually around Bonfire Night on 5 November. At this time, the leaves also begin to fall in greater numbers and the most extraordinary transformation in the entire annual cycle of a woodland takes place. On a perfectly still day, when the mist steals through the trees like a thief, I like to stop in the middle of a wood and look up for a few minutes to watch a single leaf fall. There is often a faint sound as the stalk snaps off the twig. The leaf then floats down out of the sky, spinning here, stalling there, twisting and rolling in its half flight and somehow hesitating a moment before touching the earth. Watching a leaf fall only takes a few seconds, but it is a poignant and occasionally poetic moment in the annual cycle of a tree.

This page: Trees loom through the autumn mist at Hatfield Forest, Essex. The woodland historian, Oliver Rackham described Hatfield as: 'The last wooded royal Forest in England in which all components survive: deer, cattle, coppice-woods, pollards, scrub, timber trees, grassland and fen'.

'the name is braided into the landscape just as the roots of the trees themselves are woven into the earth'

Most British place names are linguistic fossils, coined by our ancestors a millennium or more ago, to describe a place in terms of its ownership, topography, appearance, use or simply the species of tree that grew there. Thus, many of our native trees appear regularly across the map as prefixes in the names of our towns and villages. In a journey through Britain, you could visit Much Birch and Birchington, Aldershot, Elmstead and Elmbridge, Hazelwood, Yewdale, Oakhanger, Oakley and Oakworth, to name just a handful of our arboreal-themed destinations.

'Ash-' is the most common tree-related prefix, perhaps because of the importance of ash timber in the domestic and agricultural life of our distant ancestors. Ash-related place names are extant from Inverness to Cornwall and Cumbria to Essex. From Ashenhurst to Cross Ash via Mark Ash, Ashby-de-la-Zouch, Ashton and Ashbury, the name is braided into the landscape just as the roots of the trees themselves are woven into the earth.

Left: Late afternoon sunshine illuminates the slender shapes of ash trees. For historical reasons that we don't quite understand, 'ash-' is the most common tree-related prefix found in British place names.

Ashampstead means 'homestead by the ash trees'; Ashbourne, 'stream where the ash trees grow'; Ashburton, 'farmstead by the stream where the ash trees grow'; and Ashbury, 'stronghold where the ash trees grow'. Ashby, a common component of place names in the north and Midlands of England, means 'farmstead or village where ash trees grow'. Ashendon means 'place overgrown with ash trees'. Ashridge needs no translation.

Today, the extensive woodlands on the National Trust's Ashridge Estate in the Chiltern Hills, the chalk escarpment 20 miles (32km) north-west of London, are better known for beech

oak and sycamore than ash. Comprising some 5,000 acres (2,023ha) of rolling downland and woods on the Hertfordshire–Buckinghamshire border, Ashridge is a wonderful place to walk in autumn, when the mature woodlands start to colour. There is even a chance of witnessing the deer rut here, usually around mid-October. If you

are up early and lucky, you might see, in a clearing through the trees and the mist, the extravagant spectacle of male fallow deer locking horns and calling to the females.

This page: Ashridge Estate on the Hertfordshire-Buckinghamshire border is a wonderful place to walk in autumn.

The permanent, usually underground and unseen part of a mycorrhizal fungus is called the mycelium. This consists of a network of miles of microscopic, cottony, white filaments called hyphae, which increase a tree root's surface area allowing it to draw up nutrients and water more effectively. If you turn over a handful of rotting leaves in woodland, you sometimes see a velvety coating with white strands: this is mycelium. These underground fungal networks are able to establish associations with more than one tree simultaneously, allowing trees to communicate. We now understand that communities of trees are able to exchange nutrients and even information – about insect attacks, for example – via this world of submerged mycelium, which has been dubbed the 'wood wide web'.

While there are thousands of different species of fungi throughout the woodlands at Ashridge, only a handful actually produce visible fruiting bodies above ground in autumn. Of these, some are host specific – they seek out and attach themselves to select species of tree – forming the traditional associations between particular fungi and particular trees that expert mycologists and keen amateurs instinctively look for. Perhaps the best known toadstool is the fly agaric, which is most commonly found under birch trees; the alder bolete grows exclusively under alder trees; the apricot-scented chanterelle can be found under birch, pine, beech and oak trees; the birch webcap, again as the name suggests, is associated with birch; beechwood sickener, porcelain fungus and oyster mushroom are species frequently found under or on beech trees.

Picking mushrooms that you see on your woodland walks in autumn has recently become a contentious issue, mainly because gathering fungi has been commercialised in a few places like the New Forest, Hampshire. Large-scale gathering may well be detrimental to the ecology of a woodland. However, it remains acceptable for individuals to collect a few mushrooms for personal consumption. Obviously, you need some expertise to know where to find and how to identify the edible fungi in the first place, and then a good dose of common sense about how much to pick. If in doubt, consult the British Mycological Society's Code of Conduct.

Woodland fungi (clockwise from top left): Fly agaric, most commonly found under birch trees; oyster mushrooms, which frequently grow under or on beech trees; beechwood sickener, which, as the name suggests, is widespread in woods that contain beech trees and fragrant chanterelles that occur in mixed woodlands, notably under birch trees.

B eech is the iconic species of the Chiltern Hills. Formerly, many of the beech trees at Ashridge would have been pollarded – the historic woodland management practice of cutting trees back to 6–15ft (1.8–4.6m) above ground, encouraging the growth of a permanent trunk called a bolling, which sprouts new branches or poles. These branches would have been harvested every few years and used in a variety of ways.

In the Chilterns, from the mid-eighteenth century to the First World War, a huge number of beech poles went to turners, who made parts for the chair-making industry based in and around High Wycombe. Crucially, the new branches on the pollards were out of reach of the grazing animals – deer, pigs, cattle and sheep, for example – that would have shared a working landscape like Ashridge with the woodsmen.

Left: Gun-barrel straight beech trunks on the Ashridge Estate. Beech is the iconic species of the Chiltern Hills.
Above: Trunk or 'bolling' of a beech pollard in ancient woodland at Leith Hill, where Charles Darwin made frequent visits to carry out field research.
Next page: The extensive woodlands on the Ashridge Estate in the Chiltern Hills, the chalk escarpment twenty miles north-west of London, are thick with beech, oak and sycamore trees.

Like coppicing, pollarding can significantly extend the life of a tree. The famous, ancient beeches at Frithsden on the Ashridge Estate are between 350 and 400 years old. They would have been pollarded regularly for the first 200 years, to produce firewood, faggots (bundles of twigs used to heat ovens to bake bread) and poles for chair parts, as well as fuel to fire the kilns to make the bricks that were used to build the stately home, Ashridge House. The Frithsden beeches were last pollarded over 180 years ago. Today, rather than interfere with their dignity, they are left to grow – and from time to time, decline – more or less as they please.

Above: Ancient pollarded beech, one of the famous Frithsden beeches on the Ashridge Estate in the Chiltern Hills. Recently, the trees have become film stars, providing locations for scenes in various films including *Harry Potter and the Goblet of Fire*. The 'Whomping Willow' sadly died, but was at least first immortalised on the silver screen.

'The trunks could be the feet of some Jurassic monster, while their immense branches are spread like the arms of a gargantuan octopus'

It is hard not to be moved by the Frithsden beeches. They are natural wonders within reach of everyone – landmarks that represent nature at its most democratic. These trees have seen generations of humans pass by. Our history is entwined into their growth and even scored on their skin: people have carved initials and insignia into their bark over centuries. Today, the Frithsden beeches are even stars of the silver screen, providing locations for scenes in various feature films including the *Harry Potter* movies.

Hollowed, bowed, rotting in places, stooped, cracked and vaulted, these ancient trees still involve themselves in the natural cycle of the woodland that surrounds them: they burst forth with life every spring and then send their leaves down to the earth, to be converted into humus, every autumn. The trunks could be the feet of some Jurassic monster, while their immense branches are spread like the arms of a gargantuan octopus. From a distance, these great pollards are too large to read, and hard to fully appreciate. Up close, though, when you are effectively inside the fold of the outermost branches, their stature and eminence are awe-inspiring.

Left: Colossal trunks or 'bollings' of the Frithsden beeches, on the Ashridge Estate. These trees are between 350 and 400 years old.

T rees that are hollow inside, like the Frithsden beeches, provide a particularly important habitat for an extraordinary variety of residents, including bryophytes, lichens, beetles and other insects that live on the rotten wood or dry bark, as well as spiders and hole-nesting birds. In fact, ancient pollards with wood in various states of decay and a multitude of compartments can provide the environment for whole ecosystems. They are ecological treasures.

Opposite: Hollow trees provide habitats for a variety of woodland creatures while fallen and decaying leaves support whole ecosystems. Creatures of habitat (clockwise from top left): Great spotted woodpecker; delicate cobweb; spectacular stag beetle; rotting trunk of an oak covered in mosses.

Trees are described as ancient when they are unusually old for their species. Thus, a 200-year-old ash or birch may be ancient, but it takes 600 years for an oak to make the grade. For beech, a tree over 300 years old is regarded as ancient.

By accident rather than any grand design, we find ourselves with a large number of ancient trees in Britain. A combination of management practices, woodland ownership and, to a lesser extent, international trade in timber over centuries, has lead to this abundance. During much of the twentieth century, we neglected to protect and tend these remarkable trees: we cut them down, poisoned them and removed the environment they thrived in. More recently, that policy has been reversed. We are now finally coming to understand the historical, biological and cultural importance of ancient trees. The National Trust, one of the largest private owners of ancient trees in Britain, is heavily involved in their protection.

Because they need plenty of space the majority of ancient trees are found not in woodlands but in historic parklands and, occasionally, in splendid isolation. At Dinefwr Park, an 800 acre (324ha) National Trust estate on the outskirts of Llandeilo in Carmarthenshire, you can follow a walk through ancient trees inspired by landscape designer 'Capability' Brown. There are 300 oaks over 400 years old – some of which are into their seventh century – divided between the medieval deer park and the surrounding ancient woodlands sloping down to the River Tywi floodplains. In addition, there are ancient ash and lime. The oldest tree, however, is Castle Oak, thought to be some 800 years old. This giant has a girth of 36ft (11m). In autumn, you might spot fallow deer bucks with their heavy antlers, among this magnificent cast of noble trees.

Above: Sunlight and shadows drape the wooded landscape at Dinefwr Park, Carmarthenshire, home to some 300 oaks over 400 years old.

'To walk around it now, on an autumn morning
as the trees emerge from the mist,
is to transcend centuries'

Remarkably, Hatfield has changed little (apart from the aeroplanes, of course) in the centuries since Henry I declared it a 'Forest', probably around 1100. The woodland historian, Oliver Rackham described Hatfield as: 'The last wooded royal Forest in England in which all components survive: deer, cattle, coppice-woods, pollards, scrub, timber trees, grassland and fen.' To walk around it now, on an autumn morning as the trees emerge from the mist, is to transcend centuries, and arrive back in the Middle Ages. It is amazing to think that since then dozens of generations of men and women – from

kings and their courtiers on horseback chasing fallow deer and lowly peasants scavenging firewood, to famous landscape designers ('Capability' Brown worked here) and the wealthy industrialists who commissioned them – have wandered through the wood pasture at Hatfield, in many instances past the same trees, and had roughly the same sensory experience as we have today.

This page: Cattle grazing in the mist at Hatfield Forest. This unique part of the British landscape, with a variety of woodland environments, has changed little in almost a millennium and is now a National Nature Reserve.

Having survived the whim of the monarchy, absentee landlords, several notorious owners, the Enclosure Act of 1857 and the mores of early modern landscaping (many non-native trees were planted in the nineteenth century), Hatfield Forest was acquired by the National Trust in 1924. It is now managed with respect for its extraordinary history, and on account of the very rare habitat that it provides.

There is a large amount of deadwood at Hatfield, both from branches thrown down and standing dead trees, which provides important habitat for fungi and invertebrates. Healthy and diverse populations of birds – jays, green woodpeckers, great spotted woodpeckers, nightingales and kestrels, among many other species – are also present.

Left: A chestnut tree lit by autumnal sunshine, in Hatfield Forest, which is managed with respect for the rare habitat it provides.
Above: You hear the screeching call of a jay far more often than you actually see one, but the best chance is in autumn, when they are on the move in search of acorns.

> '**individual trees tussle with the wind against a darkening sky and they bend, flex, arch and sweep as each blast roars through**'

In deep autumn, when the wind is registering high on the Beaufort Scale, rotten branches get snapped off in storms and, in gales, trees can even be uprooted. Individual trees tussle with the wind against a darkening sky and they bend, flex, arch and sweep as each blast roars through. In a cauldron of noise, boughs are contorted and leaves are torn from their twigs by the hundred. Clouds of brown and yellow flecks are tossed back and forth, briefly warping like a murmuration of starlings, before being scattered on the ground.

Autumn joys (clockwise from top left): coloured leaves, squirrels gathering nuts, fungi and conkers are just a few of this season's delights.

Even when all the leaves have fallen, some trees retain a hint of their former decorative glory. Though the attention-grabbing scarlet berries of the rowan trees, the wild cherry and the whitebeam are usually devoured by flocks of birds early in autumn, other species keep their fruit through to the beginning of winter. Wild crab apples, frequent in ancient woods, hang on to their yellow-green, acidic fruit. Ash trees cling to their bunches of biscuit-brown, hardened keys well into the hibernal months when they provide a welcome source of food for bullfinches. Even a few hawthorns manage to retain the residue of their garnet berries. It is, however, the last gasp of a teeming tangle of energy, growth and exuberant life.

To visit the woods at the end of autumn is to be reminded that broad-leaved trees are constantly evolving. Our woodlands may look and even feel permanent at times – at the height of summer when the year stands still, or in the darkest, oldest days of winter – but that is an illusion. In fact, the continual process of death and renewal is at the heart of our woodland story. Autumn is the season to witness this, and to breathe in the last life of the trees before winter falls.

This page: The rich reds and browns of autumn look even more beautiful against the contrast of dark skies and frosty mornings. As George Eliot said: 'If I were a bird, I would fly about the earth seeking the successive autumns'.

WINTER

'On the last day of the world, I would plant a tree'

Place, W.S. Merwin

'When the wind blows in the woods, it is all one great swishing, swirling, sonorous sea sound'

The wind makes music in the woods, but the tune changes with the seasons. In Thomas Hardy's novel *The Woodlanders*, Giles Winterbourne could distinguish the different species of trees at a distance, simply from 'the quality of the wind's murmur through a bough.' It is an appealing thought – that a man's intimacy with these livings things can be so sensuous. It speaks of a former epoch, when trees figured highly in the lives of the majority of British people; arguably a time when our relationship with all of nature, not just woodlands, was at a more sensitive pitch.

In summer and autumn, I struggle to set apart the sounds the wind makes in the canopies of the various species of trees. I can't tell between the notes of a south-westerly giving a beech tree a broadside blast, or a northerly wind roaring through an aspen. When the wind blows in the woods, it is all one great swishing, swirling, sonorous sea sound to me, like endless Atlantic combers breaking on shingle before being sucked back out into the ocean.

Left: Looking up a tree from the ground upwards gives us a dizzying sense of how many years it must have taken to stand so tall.

In winter, however, when nearly all the trees are bare, I can identify one, very particular sound in this arboreal orchestra. Recently, walking down off the frosted heath and into Horner Wood, on the Holnicote Estate in West Somerset, the wind picked up over the Bristol Channel and I heard, from deep in the valley below me, the distinctive, staccato 'clack, clack, clack' of the bare branches of an ash tree striking one another. I stopped just inside the wood and closed my eyes against the cold wind. The clashing of ash twigs is a sound I grew up with. Like Proust with his madeleine cakes, it is something that transports me back to the long winters of my youth.

One of the delightful curiosities of the British landscape is that every wood has its own name, like the villages, hamlets and great houses they are often moored to. 'I excite myself by learning the names of the woods on the Ordnance map,' the novelist, E.M. Forster wrote in his diary in 1928, after a walk through a woodland called Honeysuckle Bottom.

Left: Winter in the woods can be as exhilarating as the other seasons. Certainly, it is as fleeting. Just when you sense that everything in the wood has finally gone to sleep, it awakes.
Above: Look carefully and you might spot a flock of long-tailed tits, a cock robin, blue tits (pictured here), a nuthatch or woodpeckers in the woods, in winter.

M any of our common woodland names
are rather more prosaic: they reference
the shape, size, dominant tree species
or historic use of a particular wood; they occur
across the countryside in a pattern, like motifs
on a quilt and underline mankind's long
association with these places. These routine

names – Long Wood, Brickyard Wood, Beare
Wood, Park Wood, Tanhouse Wood, Colliers'
Wood, Kiln Wood, Bodgers' Copse, Great Oak
Wood and Old Coppice Wood, to list a few –
contribute to the self-assurance and the innate
peace of the land in the same way the names of
our rural pubs, schools and churches do. Many

other woodland names, however, are far from commonplace. In fact, they read more like ancient, tribal incantations: Fingle Woods, Eaves Wood, Shervage Wood, Cod Wood, Pope's Wood, Dizzard Forest, Blackjack Plantation and the previously mentioned Horner Wood, are all names of woods that you will find somewhere on a National Trust property. Learning them all might have exhausted even Forster's great intellect.

Above: Bossington Hill, part of the Holnicote Estate, which was donated to the National Trust in 1944. Trees have stood in the steep-sided combes on this part of Exmoor for a very long time.

'they look like indomitable woodland heavies – the nightclub bouncers of the forest'

Horner Wood, within Exmoor National Park in Somerset, is one of the largest, unenclosed ancient woodlands in Britain. There are some 2,000 veteran trees here, dotted across the 803 acres (325ha) of woodland mantling the steep-sided combes in this beautiful corner of Exmoor. Most impressive are the muscular, pollarded oaks: with stout trunks and heavy limbs spreading in every direction, they look like indomitable woodland heavies – the nightclub bouncers of the forest. They give an air of antiquity and permanence to the wood.

Trees have stood in Horner Wood for a very long time. It is possible that there have been trees here more or less permanently since the pioneer species first colonised the banks of the Bristol Channel, when the deep cold retreated north at the end of the last Ice Age, some 10,000 years ago. That said, it is wrong to consider woodland like this as something eternal and unchangeable. Competition from other forms of vegetation, climate change, tree diseases, the unexplained habits of some tree species and, in particular, the intervention of humans, will have changed Horner Wood regularly over the millennia.

Left: Ancient pollarded oak tree, looking for all the world as if it has been coated in fondant icing as a treat for trolls.
Next page: Snow illuminates the delicate tracery of a tree's high canopy to perfection.

Today, the hue and cry of woodland industries is a distant memory in Horner Wood. The axes fell silent a century ago, when all active management effectively ended. In 1944, the Holnicote Estate was donated to the National Trust, which has since implemented a policy of minimum intervention in the woodlands. Horner Wood is now managed exclusively for nature – the same nature that has adapted to this site season after season, year after year and century after century, through endless cycles of birth and death, indifferent to changing uses and the succession of owners.

On a bitterly cold day, when my breath formed into billows of silvery ice dust, I walked off the heath that borders the wood, through the hamlet of Horner, over the packhorse bridge and up the left bank of Horner Water. There was no one

around. The sound of my boots crunching on the ancient path mingled with the gurgle of the stream. A glittering white crust covered the steep slopes of the combe. Birch trees loomed out of the mist. The frosted tree ferns covering many of the maiden oaks looked like tinsel. Clusters of brown, elliptical, winged seed vessels hung from the high branches of the ash trees. These vessels, known as keys because they were thought to resemble bunches of medieval lock keys, grow during spring and summer. In autumn, they harden, ready to be plucked from the branches and scattered by strong winds.

Above: Horner Wood, on the Holnicote Estate, Devon, is a good place to find lovers of damp, dark, places, like ferns and mosses, and all the tiny, fascinating creatures that crawl, scuttle and skitter amongst them.

Horner Wood is renowned for, among other things, the luxuriance and the diversity of its lichens. In woodlands, lichens grow on the bark of tree trunks, branches, twigs and fallen trees. They grow best in sheltered, well-lit places, particularly on ancient trees and winter is a good time of year to admire them. Because lichens extract water and nutrients from the atmosphere, many of the rare species are extremely sensitive to air quality and pollution. Thus, lichens grow in greater profusion in the woodlands of western Britain, where the dominant weather systems deliver clean air, straight off the Atlantic Ocean. That said, the drastic reduction of sulphur dioxide levels in the air in recent decades has prompted the return of plenty of lichens to woodlands and trees in southern and central England.

Lichens comprise two or more organisms – a fungus and an alga or a cyanobacterium (a microorganism capable of photosynthesis) – working in a symbiotic association. Broadly, the fungus provides shelter and mineral nutrients to the alga or cyanobacterium, which in turn provides energy from photosynthesis. Lichens are ancient organisms and they grow very slowly, taking decades or centuries in some instances, to colonise new sites. They also provide food for many invertebrates in a woodland ecosystem.

There are around 1,600 species of lichens in the British Isles, though many of these don't live on trees. Even identifying the common ones is challenging, not least because the vast majority only have Latin names. The one species that I can readily identify – oak moss is its common name – was gathered in tufts along the branches of the first ancient oak I stopped to inspect in Horner Wood. The branches or lobes, pale green above and white below, looked like a mass of tiny deer antlers. Oak moss is commercially harvested in parts of Europe, and it has been used extensively in modern perfumery. Elsewhere, on a variety of different aged oaks and especially on the larger ash trees, there was a mosaic of many lichens – blotches of yellow and white, crusts of silver and green and shaggy, grey beards hanging down from heavy boughs. Without a hand lens and a field guide, I could only admire them with uninformed wonder.

The oldest trees act as hosts to both the rarest and the greatest number of lichens – veteran oak trees can be home to 100 species or more. Sensitively managed, ancient woodlands like Horner Wood provide very important habitats, particularly at a time when these extraordinary, symbiotic associations of organisms are having to respond everywhere to changes in environmental conditions.

Left: Lichen from the genus Usnea, commonly known as old man's beard. In woodlands, lichens grow on the bark of tree trunks, branches, twigs and fallen trees, in sheltered, well-lit places. Winter is a good time of year to admire them.

You only need to walk a few hundred yards into a woodland to fall under its spell. By the time I rose back up the valley side and stopped again, the wind had dropped and the wood was mute. I leant against a rowan tree and savoured the solitude, though you are never truly alone in an ancient woodland like Horner Wood: 'Trees Be Company', as the title of a work by Dorset dialect poet William Barnes puts it. Higher up still, I looked down on the woodland on the opposite side of the valley. A grey-white pall hung close over the tree canopy along the snaking valley. Beyond, through the clearing mist, there were glimpses of Porlock Bay, the Bristol Channel and the Welsh coast.

Through the quietude, I imagined the wood in other seasons when it is teeming with fauna – red deer, pied flycatchers, dippers, lesser spotted woodpeckers, barbastelle and Bechstein's bats, wood mice and wood warblers, to name just a handful of species for which Horner Wood

is a haven. And I imagined the generations of woodsmen who might have walked up the same path as me, five centuries or perhaps a millennium ago, carrying tools to pollard an oak in the dead of winter, or to gather fuel to put a blaze in the hearth. Did they, too, pause to consider the bunches of ash keys or study the intricate detail of the frozen lichen on the broken twigs scattered across the woodland floor? We cannot know. Yet the continuity in human experience in our ancient woodlands is momentous; at times, it is even tangible. Entering ancient woodland in deep winter, one is sometimes overcome by a strange sensation – a hair-raising, numinous aura that is as beautiful as it is common.

Left: Red deer stag on a frosted heath. Red deer have inhabited Exmoor since prehistoric times. They live on moorland and use the woods for cover.
Above: Great spotted woodpeckers eat a variety of tree fruits, seeds and nuts during winter.

If you take the trouble to plant trees now, someone may walk through your woodland a century or more into the future and think well on you, even though they don't know your name. Few things in life afford such an opportunity. Of course, not everyone has a plot of land in which to plant trees. The National Trust, however, provides the chance for volunteers to do just that in various locations around the country – from the Clough Woodland Project in the Peak District, to the heathland and woodland restoration work at Foxbury in the New Forest. The single largest planting scheme – in fact, the most extensive woodland restoration project the National Trust has ever undertaken – is at Northwood, on the Slindon Estate in West Sussex. Here, a 185 acre (75ha) piece of arable land on the South Downs is being restored to woodland.

This page: Foxbury in the New Forest is the site of an important heathland restoration project. Thousands of trees have been planted by volunteers.

'Our silvicultural history, like our human history, tends to repeat itself'

Of course, the need to plant more trees in our depauperate landscape and the desire to halt the dereliction of our ancient woodlands are nothing new. The UK has had low woodland cover, at least compared to our European neighbours, since Anglo-Saxon times. Our silvicultural history, like our human history, tends to repeat itself. John Evelyn, the eminent seventeenth-century diarist published *Sylva*, one of the earliest and most famous treatises on forestry in the English language over 350 years ago, in response to many of the same challenges our woodlands face today. Then, the supply of good timber to Britain's navy for shipbuilding – a strategic necessity in the seventeenth century – was the greatest concern. Today, we need healthy woodlands urgently.

Left: We need healthy woods for a variety of social, economic and environmental reasons, and we need more of them.
Next page: You only need to walk a few hundred yards into a woodland to fall under its spell.

The tree guards and the high fence around one of the restoration sites at Northwood are to protect the young trees, mainly against deer. They are not easy on the eye, but they are not permanent either. Walking back and forth across the fields, listening to a male tawny owl hooting, I stopped regularly and tried to imagine what the space will look like in ten, 20, 50 and 100 years from now, when the sky has been crowded out. This piece of bland, gently undulating downland will be transformed into a rich, complex woodland habitat teeming with wildlife. Some of the fenced-off land will be left for natural regeneration, while in other areas, natural tree seeding is taking precedence: acorns and hazelnuts collected from neighbouring trees are being sown into prepared ground in late autumn, while field maple and whitebeam seeds are being sown in early spring.

Following the 'hoo-hoo-oooo' of the owl, I crossed the last of the fields, where the trees are being planted in clumps to create wood pasture, and walked into the neighbouring woodland called Long Beet. The owl called again. I was hoping to catch sight of him – a silhouette between the beech trees, perhaps, against the dying light in the western sky – but he was gone, to hunt the twilight in private, elsewhere. Instead, I heard, and then saw, a jay – a flash of blue, screeching through the tops of the trees. The jays, too, will play their part in the restoration of Northwood: they are important agents in the natural regeneration of oak trees as they bury acorns in autumn; when they fail to dig them up again in winter, the acorns germinate.

People seldom think of winter as a good season to observe birds in woodlands, but I sat down on a dead tree trunk, which was lying like a beached whale across the woodland floor in a clearing, to watch and listen, and to make a note of the birds I had encountered that afternoon.

Left: People seldom think of winter as a good season to observe birds in woodlands, but you certainly have a chance of hearing, perhaps even seeing, a tawny owl at this time of year.
Next page: A great flock of starlings flying towards their night-time roosting area. Starlings often roost in woods, because of the shelter that the trees provide.